Edges

Poems

by

Sterling Warner

Edges

Poems

Edges

Poems

First CreateSpace Printing 2014
Printed in the United States of America
Cover Design by Carole J. Warner
Typeset by Rose Ingold
First Printing 2012

MAPLE
PRESS

481 East San Carlos
San Jose, CA 95112
Phone: (408) 297-1000
FAX: (408) 297-2057
copy@maplepress.net

ISBN#978-1-938232-03-9

EDGES: POEMS

I
MEMORY'S MARGINS

CYBER MADONNA

Strategically stressed denim garnished by
Random sweatshop tailored holes
Adorn wafer thin sheaths
That bond practicality and beauty,
Encase the streetwise goddess's
Thighs—accentuate long legs,
Enhance airy, sylph-like movements, while
Her satin skin peeks through weathered threads
Rises above, basks through the frayed fabric's weave,
When early morning's warming rays touch
Her strapless back, kiss soft shoulders,
Bathe them in deep, moist, honey breaths.

The cyber Madonna fingers fine pearls,
Plucked from the buxom ocean's bosom,
Like meditation beads,
Gives every cultured orb an identity, blesses and
Eternalizes each mollusk's enterprise;
The world's begs to be her cybernetic oyster, so
She invites men and women to
Text her, tweet her, love her—she's horny
Longs for enduring chat room romances
As she types, her heart hangs over parted lips
Like engorged keystones above
Aphrodite's passionate arches.

Environmentally friendly lifelines
Hold their shape then creep like
Molasses along a steamy plain:
Dignified, resolute, as determined as
The sheer force of gravity,
She bends her elbows, folds her arms
Camouflages self consciousness solemnity
As loving as a preying mantis's gaze
Whose frozen posture like an invisible cloak
Becomes one with surroundings
Cautious as a vigilant caretaker
Guarding the tomb of an unsung savior.

All want to lie in the virgin's lap
While she cradles tired heads in the
Deep valley of her skirt, connecting
Without speaking, a million miles
From another's thoughts yet
United in a common denominator:
Transcendental intimacy, calculable regret; the
Madonna strokes each lover's hair that
Settles across her body as if petting
An exquisite ermine or sable stole, while
Every race, color, gender, creed, lifestyle coaxes
Another Immaculate Conception or ascension.

NATURAL SCIENCE

Miss. Maxwell, *Maxi Max* we dubbed her,
Our eighth grade natural science teacher who
Statuesquely showcased ample endowments,
Nubile young arms, tanned, toned, folded
Beneath breasts never meant to go
Unnoticed—glands best left restrained.
Womanhood personified—she taught class
Encased in silk blouses—
Provocative pink or bewitching black—
Demystified *The Origin of Species,* her Darwinian
Aplomb never trumpeted Creationism's pall, just
Teased us with bio diversity, insisted on Ecology's integrity.

Enthroned at her desk, sometimes she'd sit,
Lift an eyebrow, examine lush hair,
Pull thick auburn strands,
Curling the tips around her index finger
Let faultless tresses
Fall across her generous bosom
Never looking away—
Just doting on perfection's severity
Lost in a remembrance—an
Unsorted puzzle belonging neither to
Present day necessity nor
Nostalgia's treasured cedar chest

Full, plump, pouty lips glistened
Their luster seemed replenished as
Her tongue like treacle, parted gloss,
Licked one corner of her mouth to the other,
Created sexual double *entendres*, as each
Word she spoke would bump and grind like castanets,
Every syllable shaped, shook, and shared with
Subdued bravado, feverish intensity as,
Adolescent male and female minds
Aced Tests and quizzes, paid humble tribute
Enshrined her authoritative appeal in
Aphorisms interpreted and accepted as erotic mandates

Middle school, a time warp, carefully
Cultivated exotica experts who
Anticipated youthful awakenings
Moments when Maxi Max
Wore strapless dresses
Chaperoned our monthly rites of passage—a
Dance always held in ballroom gymnasium, just
Seconds away from sweaty locker rooms—
Damp social caverns—where each gender gathered,
Separately shared notes, practiced footwork,
Passed along hearsay imparted as knowledge,
Memorized and recited like a Maxwell science lesson.

TARGET PRACTICE

Cindy's son knew good and well
About his mother's wedding dress
Folded in a cardboard box
Nuptial vow now laid to rest.

Hidden from all sight, sound, and sense
An archery target's fabric slept
Charmeuse luster, duchesse satin
Cool as tears when silk worms wept.

The young boy'd strung Dad's bow before
Assured all suitors' fall from grace
Encouraged, Cindy's paramours
Pierced though cellulose—then lace.

Secretive sabotage seemed pure
As arrows hit romance undone
Laughter hideous fell from lips
A self-centered sprite, Cindy's son.

CANVASSING: "NO MAS"

Andrea looms large over landscapes poetic, where
Feminine mystique massages shoulders supple;
Perspiration glistening over bronze skin, trickles
      down breasts
That speak volumes about innocence unbound.

Scent of pink oleander blossoms
Overwhelms the senses, briefly
Ascends like a helium-driven psalm
      towards heaven,
Drifts miles before falling on deafening whispers.

Past lives and present vigor stream through
Veins electrified, guided like cyberspace sorties
Spurning dream spirits that glide
      across millennia
Running out of memories to reconstruct.

DESTITUTE: A CINQUAIN

Homeless
Wayward, detached
Diverts, wanders, reveals,
Faultless, nameless, guiltless, friendless,
Vagrant

ZIMS' FEMME FATALE

"You know you don't have to act with me.... You don't have to say anything, and you don't have to do anything. Not a thing. Oh, maybe just whistle. You know how to whistle, don't you...? You just put your lips together and blow."
—Lauren Bacall (from *To Have and To Have Not*)

Like Mata Hari, Nico
The Lady from Shanghai—
She entered Zims shrouded in
Mystery, misery, and malice;
Wearing seven North Beach veils,
San Francisco's Salome danced
Over to my meager dining table,
A ceiling fan breeze jostling her
Loose hair like a halo.

She sat down like she knew me,
Dampened fingers in a water glass,
Made circles around its lip 'til it
Began to sing as pure as a crystal goblet.
Exotic, distant, enticing, the
Kohl around her eyes seemed lifted from
Theta Bara's *Cleopatra,* while silver scaled
Asps enclosed arms—mystified a bedroll carriage
Befitting Gold Mountain's homeless femme fatal.

Ah, but she's gangsta, streetwise,
Sorely convinced her siren whistle and
Bling-bling would bend my knees
Pull me in her corner, make me
One of Circe's swine—sever
My allegiance to common sense,
Favor daring escapades— her
Husky inquiry resounded a clarion call,
 "Do you have a sleeping bag?"

Caution checked curiosity
'Til with one quick coy wink,
Her false lash freely fell from an
Egyptian framed eyelid; then
She let out a banshee's battle cry, a
Wail that shook all Zim's patrons
Like a San Franciscan earthquake before
SF's Salome stormed the bathroom; I paid
My bill in double, escaped a crooked desire.

Quillen's "Slip"

Disturbingly,
it sensed my face,
knew I watched spellbound by
pendulant exasperation
its confusion—its pain,
absorbed and defined a
nightmare existence.

"Slip," a fiberglass sculpture
shaped like an engorged "S"
through a looking glass . . .
eyes blinking top and bottom,
vulgar vertical lips breathing sighs,
uttering sounds:
almost inaudible,
almost sensual,
always searching.

 *"Wow-wow; low, low, low, low.
Oh no! Oh no! Where did you go?"*
gave form and measure—
meaning to its multimodal essence,
across the museum:
Grieving,
foreboding,
apocalyptic.

Maria listened—
no eyes, mouth, nostrils—just
skin draped with cascading charcoal hair.
Unpainted, like an
unfinished mannequin on canvas,
Maria could only imagine how
"Slip" appealed to all senses. Yet,
like abstract conversationalists,
they communicate.

COMFORT

Stir stick of
Unfiltered, fettered consolation
Inside a cauldron cautious
Of calamity
Like a trembling porcelain
Figurine, a moving target in a
Sharp shooter's gallery of
Pregnant ants, doing the disco thing,
Dodging pellets 'til enveloped by passion—
Giving meaning to existence.

THOTH TO ISIS

Isis, you request accountability,
Perhaps deserve an answer;
I'm pure as a virgin's bedside manner;
Gods who hang with baboons
Need no supervision to
Shape-shift on command,
Conceal desire, then eat like an Ibis.

Isis, Egypt remembers my connections
My contributions; rolling dice,
I won five extra solar days yearly from the moon
Lifted your mother's curse, provided more
Hours to menstruate in an unfertile universe
Created from dirt inside a bottle-cap; like
Cosmetics, now humans wear each age longer

Oh Isis, you know Ra's eye
Kept watching me; torn out by Set, I
Restored it, named "the whole one" Wadjet; she
Sent me a Nubian twig and beer can pull-top,
Future remnants of skyscraping pyramids;
Houses exalting material wastelands, ignoring my
Coffin Texts, supernatural spells, renewal

Isis, your birthright sinks like a
Papyrus cradle drifting down the Nile.
It's always been about personal needs
My magic gave you essence, quenched the desert thirst
While your wings breathed life into a corpse
Long enough to seed another Horus, the
Waning moon foretelling our waxing light

Isis, clutch your ankh like a holy relic,
Universe's forgotten us both;
My scribbles take flight off dusty scrolls
Crumble and fall through fingers true, when
Scales no longer distinguish the ingenuous and unworthy;
Society now devours them both in a world of feathers,
Twittering its way into a commercial afterlife.

EDGES

Albino
Peacocks spread
Cream colored fans,
One thousand blue bold
Eyes fixed like nature's centurion;
Winking galaxies amid
Twinkling puerile skies,
Three orbs outshining
Others—briefly—
Until Fall.

Then like
Molting lizards
Heaven's late hours
Shed an octogenarian
Exasperation or resolve
While starlight *chic* anew
Scales the stratosphere
Heralds glittery, majestic,
Dust-minstrels who
Wander all spring.

Love unbound
Emerges from edges,
Some explored, mostly pristine
Shelves invite cohabitating expressionists
Cast into a feathery oblivion of Art Deco motifs
Aphrodite's designs, and late August oaths;
Bonfire flames continue to blaze
Across coastal waters or
Heartfelt coral reefs
Long past summer.

II
HOMAGES

ROLLING OVER BEETHOVEN

Like a drill sergeant's gestures
arms of fleeting ecstasy
eyes glaring, glowing,
teeth grinding—grinning; the
deep pressed smile of a
lunatic—*the poet*—chants,
sweat soaked jersey clinging to
shoulders thin,
limbs feeble,
feet immobile yet
body mushrooming like
billowing smoke rings from
a thousand cigarettes
momentum gathering,
encircling, then receding:
roll it over . . . roll it over.

The poet deploys language up-tempo,
breaks into Ludwig's "Ode to Joy"
bends notes like campfire lights
flickering above willow branch canopies—
sounds, sights that hang over ponds where
Canadian geese dive into algae green—
their pastoral symphony, feathered crescendos
seductive, soothing "Moonlight Sonatas"
remain as rare as weird WWII weapons—
artillery never employed:
Flying tanks, reinforced ice ships,
winged incendiary devices
looking for rafters,
bat bombs over Japan,
napalm tied to marsupial legs
roll it over . . . roll it over

When sequestered sounds cease,
leave lipstick imprints
along roadside memories where
instrumental voices once kissed the quiet,
shattered stillness, soothed forlorn lovers;
both brought music and words back alive,
snagged hungry hearts like fishhooks,
roll it over . . . roll it over;
the kettledrum pulse
beats like a passionate pilgrim,
drives *the poet* from sanctuary's silence to
wildly wave militant arms, reading verse
as if conducting a Magnum Opus,
each a Ninth Symphony, performed
without reservation, heard without ears,
roll it over . . . roll it over.

CIRCUS OF THE SUN

Beatles in Las Vegas,
LOVE takes shape, masquerades as
Cirque du Soleil theatre:
Arms catching arms,
legs linking legs, the fab four
back to life in 2006,
forty years after the
Sgt. Pepper's Lonely Hearts Club
shook rhythm and blues at the roots,
bedrock British invader's
concept recording inspired
countless other albums, artists— on
both sides of the Atlantic—that
hit or missed like
flying trapeze artists out to entertain,
catching swinging bars at the last moment
without regret,
without net.

The Circus of the Sun
cradles spellbound spectators
revitalizes the past,
conjures Liverpool apparitions,
John, Paul, George, and Ringo, to an
palatial present venue,
showcases their likenesses,
weds original choreography to
weeping guitars and timeless tunes
—"Norwegian Wood," "Eleanor Rigby,"
"Come Together," "Let It Be"—
remastered musical might, transforms the
Mirage, home of white tiger illusionists,
creating a future mop-headed legacy where unified,
global audiences depart shoulder to shoulder,
singing, "All You Need Is Love,"
sans exotic animals,
sans Zigfried,
sans Roy.

SHEFOX

Silver Shefox still
Dazzles airway aisles;
Passion's blue veins marble
Alabaster hands that delicately
Invite all observers to
Slide into seats, buckle belts,
Observe a safety pantomime;
Some imagine her fragrant,
Lilac-scented breath
Frosting masks that drop
Indiscriminately—yet with purpose—
From secret chambers
Overhead and hang like
Pristine plastic dollies awaiting
Eager mouths and
Oxygen starved lungs.

The beverage cart mistress
Supplies thirsty sky sailors with
High altitude water, fluid that
Refreshes minds as passengers
Become liquid lotus eaters and
She morphs into Sirens, invites
Young and old on adventures,
Seductively settles everyone for
An event filled flight; yet the
Silverfox flashes a young woman's
Smile though grandmotherly lips—a
Myth-making matron,
Still green, quite alive
Despite her wintry nights,
Drawn out days, spotted
Autumn years.

The Silverfox's touches cure
More than fear of flying—
Beguiling men like Circe,
Engaging women with Sapphic charm—
This skyway attendant of many colors
Exudes exotic senior sexuality;
Hidden behind a maternal kiss while
Passengers envision her life's long journey
A mystical quest—seductress' saga—
Undaunted as Time's cold fingers
Stroke near perfect cheeks, where
Silk soft wrinkles fold like prayers—
Grace etched upon inevitable design; they
Chronicle chimerical immortality without
Apology, shaking indifferent snow globe
Wishes for eternal youth at 40,000 feet.

VETERANS

No tickertape parade
Hails their return,
Thanks their service
Presses future advantage for
Fortune's soldiers,
Alert, aloof, alone.

As lovers, their best relationships
Found shape at a distance—sustained
Through letters, text messages and twitters—
When triumph in victories
Hollow horn sounds off like shrill
Whistles and whispers flat and sharp.

From dark, damp jungles and
Dry desert plains to snow bound mountain
Peaks, we showered them with words—
Ceaseless support—while USO morale and
Special Service Programs dwindled,
Presidential visits decreased.

Old news overnight, in dreams our boys
Question blood secured prosperity and
Peace with *bayonets* and *bullets*
As Wallstreet proudly profits:
Sans heroes, *sans* freedom,
Sans liberators, *sans* home.

OMNIPRESENCE
for Rose Anna Higashi

Elegance defined, Rose Anna
Lived like activated archetypes—
Aphrodite, Athena, Hestia—
Brushing plica semilunaris from Dawn's eyes,
Absorbing lethargy's sand with sun setting sleep,
Dropping into a celestial slumber, as the Moon Lady
Rose overhead, and spread Luna's speckled ebon bliss.

Ubiquitous one, even hip girls
Placed pebbles in their shoes,
Emulated Rose Anna's carriage and demeanor
Rearranged social lives to fit her space
Admired her fashion panache, planned classes
Around her schedule—listened like apostles to
Asian, English, Japanese Literature Lectures.

Sounds of muted echoes squelch the siren song of
Rose Anna's wheels rolling up skirted stairwells;
Faithful friend, consummate beauty,
As rare and rich as poppy seed rum cake, the
Ever present sage moved in methods mysterious,
From Evergreen Valley College to St. Mary's church
Where a new flock gathers to listen, to talk, to learn.

HORSE SENSE

Literature to Legend, history through cinema
    Four-legged heroes immortalized riders
Charging oblivion, defining success, escaping disasters,
    Hooves let dust fly in followers' faces:
        Gene Autry crooned on Champion,
           An ideal equestrian mount;
        Roy Rogers straddled Trigger,
           A bold golden stallion;
        Dale Evans babied Buttermilk
           As she rode, wrote and sang;
        The Lone Ranger cried "Hi-yo Silver!" to
           "A fiery horse with the speed of light";
        Intrepid Tonto (a real Kemosabe) sat on Scout
           One fine painted palomino.
Long live Hildalgo, a painted wild mustang, who carried
    Frank Hopkins though Cody's Wild West Show;
Give a nod to Tornado, Señor Zorro's black mount bearing a
    disguised fox, who "makes the sign of the Z."

Long before western romance on the silver screen
    Where equine gallops became one's best friend and
The certain trail of attack and escape looked identical,
    Horses carried more than cowboys:
        Judah Ben Hur raced Rigel paired with three Arabians
           Defeated Messala's menacing war chariot
        Caligula's musicians serenaded Incitatus, he
           Built it a marble stable, an ivory stall;
        Alexander the Great negotiated
           Mountains atop ox-headed Bucephalus;
        Rodrigo Díaz de Vivar—El Cid—
           Died strapped to Babieca in film and legend
        Unruly "Riderless" Black Jack received distinction,
           Followed JFK's caisson and 1000 burials.
Viva Rosinante the chivalric, Don Quixote's boney nag,
    Obliging windmill attacks, de la Mancha's epic quests;
May King Arthur spur his steed, Spumador Larmi, in triumph
        During the once and future king's return to Britain.

SWAN WINGS

Spirits Lift, swan wings aloof
Phlebotomist's nightmare of
Bridal corsages and military funerals,
Caskets colorfully draped
Red, white, and blue, accented with
Friendly fire medals,
Tributes to honor, barren
Fields of iron crosses in
Lieu of flowing tributaries of life.

Hands press together, become
objects of prayer, temples of worship—
Familiar foreign faces quiver as
Eyes grieve like running faucets
Screams to silent people passing—
Countries where Collateral damage
Reaches hundreds of thousands;
Genocide masquerades as patriotism
Unleashing torrential white-water reasoning.

Fluttering limbs tremble, quiver, as
Superpower constructs promote
Democratic dictatorships,
Fling Napoleonic powerhouses against
21st century wailing walls where
Heartbeats and pulmonary attacks
Cross swords like hatred in motion, leave
Apocalyptic specters confounded, unable to
cross the rivulet under the Bridge of Dreams.

Life Could Have Been Kinder

for Susan Dobra

Life *could* have been kinder,
Susan, shaman, spirit woman,
like magic, made everyone
else seem unexceptional, yet feel spectacular;
equity shut its self-righteous eyes, thereby
swallowed whole by Chico kingmakers,
whose rings she refused to kiss,
Sustaining the publish or perish paradigm.

Life *should* have been gentler to
Susan, a caretaker, she who altered
each stream she straddled,
permitted others to become one with
her own person, one with life,
one with the universe;
east to west, west to east, Marin and the
Firmament mourn her absence.

Life *would* have been more appropriate
extending Susan courtesy;
a primum mobile, like KTAO where
"the sound of one hand clapping"
filled the night air with dappled sunshine, she
wed a smile and a whimper, laughter and tears,
makes the most of "Morning Dew" memories—
moments when the Grateful Dead salute her by name.

AFT 2012: GENERAL SESSION II

Taiko drum ensemble beats the "hara'"
Shouts awaken sleepy-eyed AFT
Convention attendees, quieting scores
Of rank and file dialogues as they try
Twisting arms of others to join causes
Support resolutions, sign petitions.
Panelists to floor debates and Q & A
Empowerment sessions, committees buzz.
Pulitzer-prize-winning journalist pontificates:
"Pensions are not gifts, just salaries
Deferred. Corporate socialism's still
Pushing back our wages a hundred years."

On the Waterfront, Market Street, San Jose
Union audience engages like rock star groupies
Fusing AFT, AFL-CIO, CFT
Workers united under acronyms.
Mantras bind: "Our State, Our Future, Our Fight,"
Fall from lips, reinforce common goals.
Delegate enclaves pick and choose moments—
Opportunities: a chance to support,
Guarded microphone minutes to oppose.
Victory's a vicious culmination:
Battlefields and bluffs where even model
AFT soldiers slump, wearily drooping,
Disillusioned by marching to compromise.

Yet after the moans, blithe laughter surfaces,
Hands first tap together lightly, then thunder;
Beyond the "bread and circuses," brothers and sisters
Speak up: "End corporate class warfare" and
"Neo-liberalism's like capitalism on crack."
Like a politic caucus—sans straw hats,
Stars and stripes, donkeys, elephants, bull horns,
Bright confetti—applause begets applause,
Feet endure endless ovations; clearly
The Old Union Hymn booms through the Fairmont
Ballrooms, hallways, and breakout sessions, all
Alliances assured a genesis:
Imminent constructive change, evolving
Arm in arm, locked in solidarity.

VIRGINIA VALEDICTION
For David, my brother

Tanbark trails stretch out like
splintered, spiritual highways from
DC/Dulles airfields to Virginian hills
where ticks pepper arms and legs,
digging in for corkscrew supper.
These days seek measurement—
Refinement—amid structural chaos,
a cosmos aligned through promise,
scientific certainty seeking emotional purgation;
the feral child within us all grasps for clues to
clarify craft and lore, honoring heritage—
suckling life span's variations .

Gazing across glassy
chocolate colored waters, a
pond where baritone bullfrogs
set nature's metronome in motion,
buzzing June-bugs quicken the pace
clicking…clicking…clicking…, and the
woods, the trees, the eastern seaboard's song
cradle cries from lonesome memories
healthy heartaches,
anniversaries that might have been,
yet remain empty fountains, fragile
unexplored possibilities.

Championing ecology, resting on religion
David quivered like an arrow through wind gusts
Arching, piercing an emerald Charlottesville meadow.
Exodus follows triumphant smiles, tortured tears,
truncated, courageous fellowships, as his life's
ripple splashes outwards,
curls like circular embraces,
moves every direction, clutches for land,
merges with twilight's chorus, *adagio,*
becomes one with the lofty landscape, till
pastoral harmonies softly fade,
leaving behind still water's wake

III
SILHOUETTES

SHAME

Shame feels like metal slag
    dragging down decency, all that's beauty,
    residing in a superficial padded cell,
    chamber whose stained walls
    recollect impure thoughts or
    unearned adulation.

Shame clothes itself in rich robes and
    exquisite imported apparel,
    hides random scars,
    covers each social lashing
    in sheer muslin dressing,
    conceals every horror show disgrace.

Shame shuffles about in honor doubtful
    like a leather trench coat dragging dust balls;
    floor-to-floor, corner-to-corner, room-to-room,
    accenting merengue dance steps,
    dignity seldom shares space with the
    mourning misfits—outside promise.

Shame rattles self-respect like
    small stone filled gourds,
    rhythmically trembling in time to
    Thor's thunderous hammer
    striking a marble sarcophagus,
    awakening its sometimes twin cousin: guilt.

Shame shatters silence like steel drum
    mallets laying down beats as calypso dancers
    energize night air, ignite the floor, explode
    vest-close confidences with TMZ aplomb,
    as noble virtues vanish—empty space
    reverberates recycled motivation.

33

ODE TO WOODEN WALLS 1978
Dedicated to The Vietnam Veterans at SJSU

—*Tôi không có lựa chọn* (I had no choice)

Wooden walls ascend—climb two stories high, house
Tar stained tin ashtrays for Vet's hand rolled cigarettes; an
Asbestos ceiling hangs tall above billowing smoke
Curling for endurance, passing through rings that seem
Afloat in every direction—each bearing the signature of a
War weary Veteran, recalling memories best forgot in
Foxhole hell or napalm nightmares—
Scars that will fester, burns that will sear
Feverish minds and scorched skeletal structures eternally:
Nóng quá, nóng quá!—
     (Too hot, too hot).

Voices heard within wooden walls resound like phantom lieutenants
Clamoring through jungle decay, above mortars shells and gunfire—
Vets who left families as liberators and returned home invisible,
Unwelcomed heroes, outsiders, malcontents, and junkies—
Tôi không hi ểu Tôi không hi ểu!—
     (I Don't Understand! I Don't Understand!)
The past's never lost in the VA present: *Am sợ hãi, Am sợ hãi*
     (I'm scared; I'm scared).
Still soldiers, they assemble like motley medieval Knights Templar,
Dismiss shell shocked tales—misguided military quest details,
Favoring frequent pilgrimages to physical therapists, psychoanalysts,
Marriage counselors, professors who try piecing dysfunctional lives together.

Wooden walls sheltered Vets like a landlocked battleship
Brushing shoulders with Tower Hall where spectral Vincent Price emerged,
Meticulous, mysterious against bellicose ivy smothering the gothic monolith,
Lecturing on art, disappearing into shadows, reemerging amid rainbows;
While on his far right, the termite ridden barricade breathed new life into
Muted conversationalists, Vietnam Vets reentering society enjoying
Extended VA benefits for South East Asian freedom fighters;
Lodged in twisted half desks, they'd carve names, companies, epithets
Chronicling forty more hours to the GI Bill, respite from recurring gloom.
Tôi bị lạc! Tôi bị lạc—
    (I'm lost! I'm lost!)

FIVE LIMERICKS
for Betty Jane Murdock

I.
Betty Jane wrote limericks well
All Peers and Professors could tell
She loved meter and rhyme
Just like any fine wine,
While her imagery cast a spell.

II.
Simplicity's love in a bind
Rapture in every kind
But beware that trite wishes
Invite insincere kisses
Seldom an untroubled mind.

III.
A true lady's quite prim and proper
No matter how tempting the offer
To leave propriety at bay
If she should go out to play
Will never allure or entice her.

IV.

One need not write limericks dirty
If you want attention at thirty
Yet it helps to be light hearted
Once recitations have started
Especially when feeling flirty.

V.

Friday we bid Murdock adieu
Treasuring everything she knew
Rejoicing life with damp eyes
Rather than pitying cries
Betty Jane lives on—let's not rue.

YULETIDE REVISITED

Hailing winter beyond
Medieval carnivals
Culturally,
Astronomically,
Religiously
Truth blinds, conjecture mutes
Sun to Son, Mithra of the
Thousand ears and *myriad eyes*
Shadows Jesus, the Nazarene

Evergreen boughs hang apple heavy;
Live and let live Christians
Adopt silhouette traditions
Align nativity with the winter solstice
Adorn tables with yuletide camellias
Dream of teaming *neeps* and *tatties*
Devour precious Christmas Haggis,
Celebrate the season, pipes a blarin',
Scotch a flowin'—anticipating miracles, dram after dram

Fragrant exotica,
Frankincense and myrrh—
Magi gifts to the *Wunderkind*—
perfumed even the rankest British stable,
Survived Cromwellian politics that
Enforced Wassail prohibition,
Revitalized Noel merriment, rejoiced with once
Forbidden Christmas geese and mince meat pies,
Cinnamon dusted with cloves, nutmeg, and spices.

SHADOWCAT

Quiet curtains, silent doors
Empty windowpanes—no face
Looking out, peering in—
White paw pressing under sills
Gone like drawn shades,
Sylvester, the ShadowCat.

Mouthing words as soundless as his
Byzantine silhouette against curtains
He swaggered into rooms wearing
Dusty spider webs like masques
Across his face, proud, defiant,
Elegant as an Egyptian adornment

The Ebony ShadowCat would
Push open doors, stick furry feet under sills,
Sun himself under a green desk light
Curl inside my leather briefcase—
Just his size, just his style—pause as
Carole arranged the Sioux blanket just so

A Bamboo bustle chair enveloped Sylvester
Like protective cradle arms, a palatial crib
Where tap-tapping clawless paws
Kneading attention—some loving—stretched in
All directions as he patiently supervised our actions
In shadows, watching, waiting, whispering comfort.

FORTUNE'S CHILD

We knew she'd be a child forever,
derailing her brother's toy train with
jelly beans and bobby pins,
pulling synthetic hair from her
sister's Busty Barbie, hiding
headless dolls under feather pillows;
mad but motherly,
connecting need and circumstance
she hooked up with a
Belleview orderly, bore his son,
held the baby to her breast until
social services confiscated it—her
greatest achievement—and then
disappeared after its father got fired for
sexual harassment—around the same time her
insurance evaporated, eliminating post-natal care.

Some say she kept house in a
condemned condominium;
slept in squalor's habitat empty for years,
where sounds still linger:
pet paws tap-dancing across linoleum,
urinals flushing, water running,
pilot lights clicking on, turning off
Winter, Spring, Summer, and Fall;
"to everything there is a season,"
or so a book promises, yet
when rooms come alive with
the adult-child's songs, it seems as if
all become trapped in a singular moment, where she
clings to near impossible deliverance like a lottery winner.

Convalescent Cub Scouts: A Choka

Toes spread then freeze, like
Neck hair stiffened by cold winds,
Bare bottoms that nest
On rotated mattresses
Or icy bedpans,
Each day is night, each night is day;
Daily visitors
Range from family to strangers,
Lawyers to lovers,
Who humbly pay their respects,
Speak through thick bed bars,
Or overstuffed rec. room chairs,
Endearments unknown,
Faces often forgotten.
I came with cub scouts,
Our intensions most noble,
Brought homemade treasures—
Gifts for those who imagined
Us other people,
Like magi on a journey;
Rubbing alcohol
Scented rooms like rarified
Airborne smelling salts;
Odors we'd associate
With old people and rest homes;
Cub presents made eyes water,
The crude work brought joy
Our furry pets caused delight,
Tactile strokes renewed their lives.

Memento Mori

In hoc memento mori,
Embossed Emblem etched above an
Pentagram insignia, Sir Gawain's star—
Solomon's sign—five straight strokes
Draped across the quillion that
Forms one interlinking scar;

Art edges its way forwards, blinks
Backwards glances, never viewing,
Seldom reassessing or regretting
Yesterday's creation or this morning's news,
Weighing Vanity's worldly merit
Against Salvation's Divine Possibilities;

A Reaper lives behind every dumpster, a
Scavenger whose forte sleeps with social harvests
Where unwashed arms toss Goodwill garments
Into the air that plummet like lead confetti
Blanket the barren terrain with motley colors that
Paint slopes, designate elevation, offer topography;

Street punks and white-collar crooks walk the same path
Wait like patient phone callers placed on hold,
Transient life advances towards inevitable closure where
Dross verbiage—deceptive jive and opaque jargon—
Privileges no one; earthly titles lack prestige, since smiling
Death scoffs at people who forget—or deny—mortality.

PIPPA'S PHOTO: A CONVERSATION

Pippa please
Write me a choka
Where syllabic precision
Falls as eloquently as
Your figure hugging dress at
Sister Catharine's Royal wedding:
Pure, pristine, promising,
Somewhat familiar.

Come ruffle my hair
like a fussy mother,
Peck at my cheeks
As a doting sister, then
Kiss my lips hard and long
Like an ageless lover;
Each I take in stride...
All fulfills a need.

Pippa do let your
Seductive locks cascade
Across demure shoulders,
Like brunette waves
Gently rolling over your body,
Each subtle movement a
Fashion statement, every party or
Tritely spoken word, front-page news.

INKED

For Cathy

Tanizaki's Seikichi, a "tattooer" who
enjoyed slinging ink, pounding skin,
grinding out samurai tribal tats,
found a young geisha's back an ideal flesh canvas—
perfect and pure for his magnum opus,
a fiery black widow spider and her prey wreathed in flames,
a design where he emptied his tortured soul, poured the
mysteries of his craft, lost the secret of artistic distance,
victimizer becoming victim of his own invention.

Ask Lyle Tuttle, talk to Tala, speak with Shadow:
tattoo lovers hear art calling, respect beauty beckoning;
curiosity and intrigue push taboos aside; amorous
arms open wide, inviting every bee-sting embrace
look to the ink envisioning ornamentation, change:
koi fish that swim down spinal cords, alluring
tramp stamps, rainbows, roses, knots—
accepting each irresistible prick as an
affectionate electrical stroke.

Tat enthusiasts become decorative meat, healing projects:
mottled *sleeves* needled with kaleidoscope orchids,
reptiles, amphibians, mammals, fairies, fauna—
irons kickin' it into third while some
remain silent cadavers, faultless, pulsating fabric—
blank slates that ignore angry skin—other Michaelangelos
chatter like Snow Monkeys, demanding "purple passion,
"Aztec yellow," "victory red," bonsai blue," driving body
engravers crazy with pseudo-expertise and preference.

Jubilant eyes shut as tight as bolted castle gates,
hold onto their quest, grimacing yet smiling
above all else, resolute while the Tattooer
violently caresses shaved skin gone crimson
piercing unpigmented pores as
lightning-bolt biceps cease to throb or
discriminate between the pain and pleasure
pumped into each permanent creation—
a fertile holy grail amid Lubriderm blessings.

IV
ARABESQUES

CHOICES

"Indifference and neglect often do more damage than outright dislike"
—J. K. Rowling

Oh Aunt Angie, there's one thing that's certain,

Stardom's glamour inspired you to roam;

Your gifts—most material—still hurt one,

Cousin Glenn grew in a motherless home.

Oh Aunt Angie, why do you gasp and sigh?

Did the city of lights pay no attention?

Perhaps you've charcoaled your brows too high,

Or Hollywood's thwarted your great ambition.

Angie, Angie, what now seems to matter?

You've had all the breaks yet growl like a bear,

After celluloid contacts all scatter,

A broken family's quite hard to repair.

Regret's natural, amends never sure,

You severed trust once you walked out the door.

SIX TANKA TENORS

I.
Dawn's May mists lift while
Spring awakens young bodies
Half-clothed on the moor;
I want to grasp shadows past—
Cast as bright constellations.

II.
Capitola beach
Shells, kelp, jiggers commingle
Toes dig deep wet sand;
Damp August t-shirts cling to
Young lovers playing at dusk.

III.
Harpoon horizons
Watch whaling apparitions
Glide to Nantucket;
Oil drums filled, scrimshaw pipes lit,
Sailors dream of Rapunzel.

48

IV.
Dragonfly magic
Atop slender bamboo shoots
Spring showers quench thirst;
Rejuvenated lives move
Forward, yet return to dust.

V.
Twilight forms merging
like harpsichord concertos
escape fall dust, winter winds;
physical young girls and boys
become one like their elders.

VI.
When spring blossoms bloom
May Queens and Kings consummate
Desire with love;
Eternalizing moments,
Anxiety shifts concerns.

TAXIDERMISTS

Reanimaters,
Illusion's masters,
Taxidermists strive to fulfill
Hunters' fantasies—miracles
Performed on pheasants blasted
By double barrel shot guns,
Grizzly bears with
Badly damaged capes, or
Deer, elk, and moose
Shot in fields
Wrapped in ragged hemp ropes that
Rip fur from roots;
Sports men and women proudly
Drag quarry to roadside vehicles,
Scrape hairs from hides
Strap each carcass
Atop hoods or tossed
Indifferently into dingy truck beds.

Hands mold clay
Around glass eyes,
Stretch pelts over fiberglass
Forms, small and large;
Oil and acrylic paints regain
Definition in mouths cracked and
Dried from the kill, the tanner, and the
Taxidermists who breathe visual
Life into preserved outer shells of
Nature's fowl, fish, and fauna
Where they lurk in museums,
Trophy rooms, science halls,
Bar tops and living room mantles,
Each point on every
Rack of antlers—an
Exaggerated display of
Buck sexuality—polished,
Lacquered, preserved.

QUILLEN'S "SLIP" #2

Written in response to Melissa's San Jose Museum Writing Prompts

It sensed my face, knew I watched spellbound by its confusion—its pain, absorbed and defining a nightmare existence. "Slip," a fiberglass sculpture shaped like an engorged "S" through a looking glass . . . Eyes blinking top and bottom, vulgar vertical lips breathing sighs, uttering sounds *almost* inaudible, *almost* sensual, *always* searching.

"Wow-wow; low, low, low, low. Oh no! Where did you go?" gave form—meaning to its multimodal essence, grieving and apocalyptic. Across the museum, "Slip" wails to Maria—woman without eyes, mouth, nostrils—just skin draped with cascading black hair. Like an unpainted, unfinished manikin on canvass, Maria only imagines how "Slip" appeals to all senses, yet like an abstract conversationalist, she communicates as well. Both endure.

HAIKU CROSSROADS

Casting nylon lines
Piercing salty ocean depths
Hooks grasp seaweed, fish

> Unwashed face sleeps on
> Feather pillows—new straw beds
> Simplicity's cradle

Waxing moon conjures
Sweet Jamaican fantasies
Romanticized sloops

> Dry ice cells hover
> Autumn phone calls unanswered
> Dead zone lovers kiss

Saunas and soak tubs
Moisten lizard skin tissues
Soothe wintery bones

> Drawing attention
> Bleeding color carousels
> Springtime pantaloons

LIMERICKS

THE WEDGE BOARD

There once was a pottery master
Who poured a wedge board of plaster
    Using hands to break bubbles
    was the start of her troubles
And the result is now a disaster.

LIMERICK DIET

A beautiful woman named Jenny
Dined less and less to become skinny;
    Eating nothing but fish
    She quite soon got her wish
But can't even wear a bikini.

DR SEUSS

Burnt Toast and marmalade jam
Tastes great with green eggs and ham;
    One must thank Dr. Seuss
    Without being obtuse
Cool and collect as a clam.

STAR DAZED

I'm truly a babe don't you think?
I sing, and I dance, and I drink;
I'll know where to start
Once I get the lead part
And sign my new contract in ink.

THE PLAYER: A DIAMANTE

Flirt
Playful, wistful
Smiling, winking, alluring
Sensual fingers encircle wineglass
beckoning, teasing, enticing
Healthy, wholesome
Coquette

'SKYPEIN' WINDOW

Written in response to Melissa's San Jose Museum Writing Prompt

"I saw the best minds of my generation destroyed by madness, starving hysterical naked . . . " Yes, Ginsberg, I heard your words as I observed the "Awakening in the City." Each window showcases naked bodies—all very much alike—at work, play, or both. Breasts hang over computer keyboards; fingers move through cyberspace, take sky clad explorers to new frontiers and as well as familiar old ones. Torsos link- lock in orgiastic rituals; nude maestros "tickle the ivories;" men and women play doctor; undefined faces fixate on glass tubes; bodies stand by windows and engage in early morning exercises, flashing the world. Buxom babes and buffed dudes sit around conference call tables, still naked; their eyes remain glued to the electronic wall-screen where other bodies in the buff pontificate—set the world right. The *bona fide* collusion of *Skypein* grotesques enjoy breakfast-like company, the commonality between the colorful caricatures beyond fabrications of social rank. Joined hip to hip in a common lunacy, mutual psychosis, they nonetheless clothe themselves when they sleep.

SKIN AND SCULPTURE

Television never lies:
naughty nurses testify
their Brazilian butts and
perkier boobs never felt better
when pressed against
shoulders, chests, calves, thighs of
cosmetically enhanced lovers.

Males return favors with solid
silicone pectoral implants,
excite imaginations through
abdominal etchings, create an
illusion of six-pack abs which they
showcase proudly, wearing thin,
tight T-shirts three sizes too small.

Kudos to culture's superficial aesthetics;
looped for hours each day and every night,
thirty-minute info commercials
preach the "good word" for
busty wanna-be or buff disciple whose
Viagra promises virile possibilities, exploits
uncompromised by muscle building steroids.

AIRPORT MENAGERIE

Airport porthole
Reveals a cultural
Cornucopia, the
Minor buying Fritos
>Dresses like
>Heidi of the Alps, while
A college coed hangs
Awhile in deep deliberation,
Determining which dairy product,
Best complements her figure.

On the closest seat to Gate B-23
Headed nowhere, a physical therapist
Dramatically waits for her
Delayed flight to resume,
>Touches herself, relaxes knotted tension,
>Bona fide and imagined,
Hums old Leonard Cohen tunes,
Falls into slumber; child star brushes past,
Expects to oblige her with an autograph,
Meets an indifferent, celebrity consciousness.

Final call—flight 699 to Chicago—
Stragglers avoid punctual, uneven
Lines that move like arthritic snakes;
The paralegal cougar
>Shuffles past the locked cockpit,
>Walks as if Madonna—without
A prayer or a song—left
Hand dug deeply into her boy-toy's
Front pocket, youthful trophy
She claims as her own.

V
NIGHT-HAWKING

GYPSY SEA

Sunrise: necks stretched out like hungry clams
Lurch for the Ibuprofen emperor
Whose numb fingers wave loners to café chairs—
Rivet them to sticky alligator seats, bottom sides
Textured with chewing gum madness; daydreams
Pull life's canopy over sand and foam,
Seasick tides lick each empowered undertow
Sheer bag luck burlesques diffident efforts,
Tête-à-tête conversations revealing
Epiphany-like promises through opaque glass.

Nightfall: along the coastline, bonfires blaze
Bodies gather, mouths breathe desire, minds re-imagine;
Moving between cosmic and material worlds,
Cleaving mustard greens like an armful of roses, a
Gypsy mystic dances like a whirling dervish
Toe-ring magic fractures limestone bones
Unbrushed by feet for millennia
Bangle bracelets—silver cymbals rouse
Ever vigilant, sleepy-eyed centurions
Stand guard over her Technicolor Roma.

Astronomical dawn: dropping arms signal nocturnal closure,
Dancing legs and burning feet cease
Rhythmically rocking shellfish strongholds;
Dense auburn moss calmly spreads its way south,
Wraps a tranquil riverbed in nature's sheath,
Guides an *Arabesque* estuary toward a
Salt water *Fiord,* lateral moraine, where
Nourished sediment dwellers burrow home
High tides pull ashes, bathe shorelines
Littered with seaweed, driftwood, memories.

ECO FENRIS*

As autumn leaves swirl above cobblestone walkways,
Tiny tornados suck gravel and grit into vortices and
Like long green hair tuffs
    jutting from an old man's ear,
Aggressive grass grows between bricks and stone,
Encroaches upon grey cement lines—fractures
That define a tired, time-tested spine,
    osteoporosis case study,
Arching in every direction along a
Thin vertebrate column upholding
Our earth mother's only back, whose
    disks we dare not tread on.

Are these the shades of quality time?
Daylight peeping Toms in the guise of law and order
Restraining an ecological Ragnarok
    like a 21st century Glepnir,
Magically forged from the feline footfalls, bird spit,
Fish breath, mountain roots, and a woman's beard;
Surreal camera lenses capture
    melting leaves on laurel wreaths
As Fenris wolves all around us gnaw—escape ribbon shackles
Maypole dancers exchange apricot kisses, trade their
Diamond studded designer nails for
    Blue Blocker shades or 3D glasses.

---

*   Fenris, son of Loki, was a huge wolf of Norse Mythology whom the gods bound to a rock with a magic chain (crafted by dwarves) called "Glepnir." Prophecies declared that when Ragnarok (end of the world) occurs, Fenris would escape its bonds and devour Odin, ruler of Asgard (home of Norse Gods and Goddesses).

ROAD SHOW

Art

Deco

Cameos,

Watch fobs,

Ankle bracelets,

Antiques piled high

On judgment's tables:

Diamond tiaras, toy trains

Elgin timepieces, pensively

Await authoritative assessment,

Drop dead auction prices, while

People compare treasures from

Whiskey decanters to

Tambour desks, or

Alleged artistic

Masterpieces

Purchased

For mere pennies at

Blowout yard sale bargains or

Happenstance hoarder

Giveaways.

Pop

Culture cashes in,

Raises its arrogant head like

A spitting Cobra lost in a trance,

Swaying, dancing to the rhythm of

Twenty-first century charmers,

Forked tongues replaced

By ceramic studs,

Tramp

Stamp stencils,

Serpentine armbands,

And gold belly button rings;

Road show aficionados

Flaunt

Up skirt photos of

Tinsel town celebrities or

Rock star possibilities

In everyone of us—

Panting, pining for

Fame's fifteen

Minutes.

PERSEPHONE

Pomegranate seeds and cherry cola
Make each Persephone a happy sovereign,
Underworld ruler, Hades' queen,
She plays victim and virgin with equal aplomb:
Demeter's daughter weeps, while the
Earth mother mourns their broken bond,
Goddess neglecting to plant, fertilize, harvest.

Persephone, I'd love you
If you didn't need it both ways
Step outside regal comfort zones
Plant one on me at unguarded galas
Get used to set-ups, shakedowns,
Useful hours amid wasted moments
Life's midnight vigils, minutes of repose.

Persephone please, pause, ponder, reflect
Leave the anger, keep the passion;
Swallow sorrow a thousand times,
Spit out sidewalk possibilities, quit
Your life of sheltered compromises—
Fortune's friendly backside—and
Allow a daily fresh facelift.

NETWORKING WARRIORS

I.

Bagpipes and trumpets
    Belt the Blues like
        Barbershop quartets
    Ringing cords strained,
Harmonies out of key
    Circles of fifths claimed
        By patrolling DJs
    Clad in fatigues, who
Pace naked hallways
    Resist the definition of
        Rap music as disco's
    Enduring revenge—or that
Internet graffiti survives for art sake.

II.

Pedestrian leaders
    Conscript digital
        Media militias,
    Equipped with cameras
Cell phones, computers,
    iBooks, and droids;
        High def armies
    March rank and file,
Rallying against
    Rupert Murdoch
        Despots until the
    Common enemy's crushed—
Regrouping to identify another foe.

VAMPIRE AMORE

Adolescent boys
love Dracula's brides
Sexy Vampires in
white chiffon,
floating across crypts,
moving like mist
chilling the air,
stirring young hearts that
romanticize drawing
bloody crucifixes on
rounded breasts with
undulating cleavages,
mysteries of
the night.

Like lampshades
channeling incandescent fog
onto luminous rutted ceilings,
Vamps stay awake late,
clinging to evening's blindness,
celebrate Nosferatu's rise,
listen for screeching hinges;
undead footsteps
like silent cat paws,
quicken their pace—
escape past orgiastic catacombs,
mausoleum manacles,
where resting places become
lively tombs 'til dawn.

SMITTEN

Tongues touch tongues
Dart in and out like vipers,
Roll under, over, around—pierce through
Eager, mutually consenting mouths,
Pores open; moisture collects,
Liquid diamonds in the rough
Dribble down cheeks,
Anoint flushed faces like holy water
Pass over lips, travel down chins
Kiss skin like a string of pearls or
Hang there like jeweled garlands
Dreamy quixotic rationalists, lovers
Venerate animal ecstasy, disguised as
Eternity's tender passion, plunge dark
Recesses of each other's heart

Shoulders sigh as
hands massage, magically
Hitting their mark in fortuitous moments
Multiplying bliss into
seventh heaven rapture where
euphoric exaltation invites replication
Bodies curl in fetal position,
Minimizing microscopic space between
Satisfied souls still rocking with
Rhythmic, suggestive sanctity
Baptismal floodgates release sensual torrents
Drench initiates, bless simple ceremonies
Launch them into experiential frontiers where
Inductions resist neglect, as
passions purify promises.

DRIVE-IN CHOKA

Legs rock in rhythm
Karmann Ghia back seat fun
Summer drive-in date;
Movie summaries studied
Before couples park,
Memorizing each plot line;
From early May moons
Until late August sunsets,
Air cooled upholstery
Cushion eager spring bodies,
While exhaling lungs
Fog up the clear car windows
Lust reigns unrestrained;
Restless minds coached and caressed
Unite ambivalent hearts.

INQUISITION

Tell me what it means as tender touches cease,
embraceless days dancing on tailcoats of night,
where promise escorts impoverished libidos,
linked arm and arm, pulse to pulse;
flickering flames and detached luminescence
consecrate satisfaction's future with
repackaged lip ambrosia
reduced to kisses on the cheek.

Teach me to interpret awkward silences as downcast
eyes rivet themselves to crimson oak knots that blink
like ebon orbs weeping, tears falling, mascara running
indifferently between the tongue and groove,
uniting the hard wood floor planks whose solid timbers
creak feeble defiance at softly padded footsteps,
raise righteous indignation to spiked heels and steel soles,
become expanding giants during blind midnight hours.

Remind me how it feels when young minds mature, yet
time rapes mobility, and minimizes commotion,
Nighthawks who substitute ballrooms, "clubbing it," and
late night cafés for stately, determined,
checkerboard flirtation and twilight bridge partners,
stepping out for frequent hospital visits and funerals
that strike a chord with impermanence—sometimes
welcoming closure as divine intervention.

IMPERIAL SONNET

Rasputin lingers in the star clad night;

When autumn winds still blow, shadows embrace,

Lust rich desire exudes wrong and right

Vodka breathing kisses no-one can trace.

Past curtains, hallways, courtyards, every door

Runs Anastasia, not looking back;

Who has honored royals? No one's quite sure;

Under Faberge's a fatal crack.

Haunting young Romanov and her jewels,

Death set the Grand Duchess' trousseau aside;

She sought life from Cossacks, peasants and fools,

No Catherine the Great, her innocence died.

Hell fire ne'er consumed this child of the Tzar

She's been seen with Elvis walking afar.

Sterling Warner

Over the last 30 years, Sterling Warner has taught a wide variety of Creative Writing, Composition, Literature, and Rhetoric courses at two and four year colleges and universities. Warner's fiction, non-fiction, and poetry, works include *Thresholds* (© 1997); *Projections: Brief Readings on American Culture* (2nd edition © 2003); *World Literature and Introduction to Theatre* (5th edition © 2008); and *Visions Across the Americas* (8th edition © 2013). His poems have appeared in many literary publications, including *The Chaffey Review, In the Grove, Faculty Matters, Leaf by Leaf, The Messenger, The Monterey Poetry Review, inside english,* and *Metamorphoses* – as well as the *NCTE/TYCA Poetry Month Celebration Archive.* Additionally, Warner has written three collections of poetry: *Without Wheels* (In the Grove Press © 2005); *ShadowCat: Poems* (Maple Press © 2008), and *Edges* (Maple Press © 2012), as well as *Memento Mori* (Maple Press © 2010), a chapbook. A Hayward Award winner (2000), Warner currently teaches in the English Department at Evergreen Valley College, where he has served as the Creative Writing Program Director, The Evergreen Valley College Author's Series Organizer, the *Leaf by Leaf* literary magazine Chief Editor, and the Evergreen Valley College Annual Spring Poetry Festival Coordinator.

Sterling Warner

72

www.ingramcontent.com/pod-product-compliance
Lightning Source LLC
Chambersburg PA
CBHW071927020426
42331CB00010B/2762